The Wilderness and Tea Poems

ISBN: 978-1-716-91863-6

The Wilderness

Om Tara Tu Tara Ture Soha

Big Creek drops down effortlessly,
Cutting repeatedly through the deep echoes
Of original harmony,
And in each fragment given heart
Her energy forces a few holistic interventions
From the granular hemispheres
While the Owl slumbers and dreams
The moments passed just before the light.

I, some isolated moments walking
While you so vast are passing
Ten billion times beyond the waves
Of my confined perceptions
Changing through the sounds of this free falling river
Within the wind marked only by its passing
Around the trees and grass and canyon slopes
Where rocks cast off their mothers' faces
Have charged toward the river
And stopped where force has left them
Piled in a heap
Beneath their parents' chip-marked faces
Battered by the rites
Of larger waves of weather
Cast off the Owl at night.

And I would choose a future
Sitting by this creek

Soaking tired feet
Beneath
This tumultuous rattling
Of leaves,
And I would climb these canyons
Above this basin path
Where clumps of brown-green grass
Bunch beside the trails of sheep,
And I would sit on ridges
Above the blue-green Gorge
And ancient blood-red markers
Painted by Shoshone
In the passing of the sun,
And…
I would spend my life
Watching Big Creek burn
In moments roused by earthy shifts
Rippling through passing times,
Your hand held by mine,
A universe of moments,
But the Owl dreams before me,
Beyond my wishful prayers,
In isolated moments
Beyond the rasp
Of our more mortal passions.

Dessverre

Oh, take my hand now, Life,
And gaze into my eyes
By Big Creek's hallowed side.

Ahh, the past is but a woven night

Before our Truth is brought to light.

Let our eyes wonder as we walk along.
Let the fear of moving forward loosen.
Let in the light of this day's morning sun.

It is our time to go.

Many feet have pressed these rocks
Where we are now afoot:
Yes, many walked this trail
As fragments in the past,
And if some prints were matched with ours,
Their prints would surely ware
The stones beneath our feet,
And any ware that changed such stones
Our feet might never meet,
But if our feet were matched
With walkers of the past,
Would we change such change
As they by chance had cast?

I don't have the answers,
For in isolation I have roamed,
Caged from all outside,
Captive,
Restrained from all within,
Blinded.
All now is but a raging on.

Here, Big Creek falls along,
Marking time's vast passing
In missing memories,

The trail melting in and out of sanctuaries
Far more than musings,
Ecologies of melting moments,
Never at a still point,
Never timeless,
Always joining our own chiming
And other walkers' thoughts,
Some in blessings
Others not
And all just
Before the questioning
Lost in memory's falsehoods,
A past clockwise counter woven
Twixt strands of facts
From acts in random
That unify the present
And bring possibility
To our future.

Let us wander, now, not in a rose garden,
But in a garden full of flowers petaled black and white,
Where I in intersection
Lived a past
Dreamt in restless isolation,
Lasting for some moments
Composed of countless fragments,
Perceived
And unperceived
As day discovers distance
Upon this hardened trail we now traverse,
A trail full of spirits mingling in the bliss
Of thoughts brushing through my mind,
Thoughts…

Folded by a Hellish baker
With fangs and claws of steel
Into gruesome clarity,
Into a ship bobbing upon the ocean,
Cast by winds to isles
Where Spain had left her
Cannons stored in stone
And Kerberos screamed in rage,
A place where, like Achilles,
I ran reborn
Singing by the shore,
"I am stern, acrid, large, undissuadable, but I love you,"
With that love set in cacophonous city sounds
Where children doves for shinnies,
Cast from high above
To ladies in white dresses who waved from
Sinking boats
Upon a poisoned creek
That flowed into an ocean
In comatose repose,
A place where spirits sang of woe
And shadows danced on stages
Beyond imperial sights
For soldiers brainwashed within the might
Of one clear truth presuming right,
A place seeming supportive of the strong:
The manning
Passing spilling seeds to those waving
From their wooden boats,
To those women and children
Forgotten and then swept below
Bridges built of stone.
It was a place where smoke of gray and white and black

Would curl and twist and wrap restless
Between streets and structures,
Sluggish and musty, yet musing in decay,
Smoke rising above the coals and embers
From which it sprang
To unfurl, hiss, and spit
At soles sold and music played,
Smoke drifting and winding through windows
Void of glass
Where men and women sat
In a miasma of flags and colors and cackling,
Their arms
Intertwined,
Eyes of white,
Pupils rolling back,
Smoke that climbed higher still,
Toward the darkened sky
And starless night,
To drop much faster than it rose
And, after, to slither down windless streets
On nights that trapped
The city's paltry air and sounds
Beside the auction blocks.

Oh,
The auction blocks exist,
And I have seen the slaves,
And I have been there marching
Across that languid land
Where spirits cried in anguish
And eyes extended hands,
Where incense kept the bugs at bay
While muscles arched taunt and tight, skin glistening

In moonlight beams' glowing gaps
Made of door-less doorways in plywood rooms where
sweaty splashings
Fell on packed-dirt floors,

And I refused the sweathouse voice that
Boiled from the rocks,
And I forgot the men who sang the wordless songs,
And I forgot the thunder made within the clouds,
And I became a feather that danced upon the ground.

Oh, who shall come from the offspring of
My offspring in distant centuries?
And will my youth forsake them
As they in singing pass?
Are my daughters auctioned within the wanton music
Of money changing hands?
Are my sons in chains with shackles round their necks?
And what of my offspring's infants, and
Further down the trail,
What of those whose future is forgotten
By countless armies passing upon that
Mystic petaled ocean
From which this night was ripped in birth?

Oh, Guilt!
Oh, Shame!

Minos! Minos! Wrap your tail no more!
These prisoners scratching at my falsehood woven
Leave bloody nails embedded in some coffin
Six feet beyond
This wilderness.

Once upon a time, a lady gnarled, wrinkled,
Flesh clinging to her bones,
Torn by pains of dreams forgotten,
Watched the blocks within a bar
As her children dancing danced
Across a blood-red floor
Beneath a flood of floral patterns
Dripping from the walls.
And she, savvy in her years,
Began to speak for hearing
Where I was often found.

"These piles of rice
Set here and here and here
Are that remains
At bottom's heap,
Below nations and these
Painted paper plates.

On each plate now mounded white
That makes in whole a witnessed might,
Each grain seeming steaming, but
More… a single light,
A whole within our sight.

See, in this single grain, a moment shared?
Here, in this grain
Is food to quench forthcoming hungers,
Food to finish work,
Food to open eyes,
Food for findings found
On plates of white."

(Ahh, Christ!)

"And in each grain, I've gained that strength
My years of suffering need
That I might lift my morning's bed
And place it safe away,
For this rice will feed me
Give me freedom,
Give me riches in starvation,
So on this grain,
Now, is perfume
Left on fingers
From morning's use,
And off this grain
Upon my hair
I wipe what excess still remains
That those who eat from heaping plates
Will see the peace within our grasp."

Thus she spoke of rice
In mornings after bathing
Or afternoons beyond the warmth
Of humid human days
Blistered by the sun
Before the bidding blocks began
To bustle and wiggle as worms and
Bugs crawled through fleshy orbs
Now doorways to gardens and windows to the past,
And to boiling days and smoky nights
She spoke speckled moments planned to hatch.
Beneath the dripping walls
A mother…at least of sorts…she became,

Her son, a brother,
And daughter to a sister same
As blood ties blood in grace.

My brother shared his mother's rice
With wife and children born
And bathed his feet in muddy streams
Beyond those screaming in the night.

Two thousand apenecks unleashed:
The suffering set upon the suffering
To lead the suffering.

His mother fluttered from the tree,
While the nightingales danced within the limbs
And leaves.

Apenecks charging across blood-red floors,
Searching sweaty beds,
Screaming in confusion
At the birds beyond their reach.

Rice was spread
About the ground and water stains
From joyous tears
Spilled from aching eyes.

Nightingales moving in morning's light:
Suffering cleansing suffering
To continue suffering.

His children
One by one by one

With bloated bellies fell.

Apenecks, tired of the chase,
Were washed by singing birds
Woven to a patterned flow
Dripping down the walls.

He fed them rice
And watched them die
Withing his thinning arms.

Apenecks left
Thinking to return
When day became the night.

Charms within the stream
To prison led his feet,
Caging him within a muddy, muddy jail.

Apenecks filled the streets.
Some bought charms that night
To speed their beating hearts
And dull eluding minds
From the fact of slaves
In darker plight.

The rain fell and fell,
Water dripping
Between bamboo leaking
Above his hole filling.

An apeneck watched a slave
Standing on a block,

**Unknowing of Her children
Breathing mud and scattered rice.**

A man in black and green
Threw a plate of rice and fish bones
Into a hole
Holding that brother breathing
Water, mud, and night.

**An apeneck caught a nightingale
And wondered at the chains
That jingled as they danced
And danced between the bars.**

(Om, Tara, why are people not affected
By nightingales?)

My sister…
In childish grace
Would dance across the floor
For ecstasy of life…
Eleven and spinning widdershins twirling,
A lark above the strife.

Oh, sister's hair laid long
Between gravity's strong pull below
And Universal mass above
Fanned out beyond her spinning moments
In the black wave of her youth,
And she would dash across the beach
Below the bidding blocks

And drippings from the walls,
And I would toss her Pesos,
Silver shinnies,
Falling,
Glinting,
Spinning,
And then landing
on
the
wet
sand.

I Loved a little sister who danced across a stage.
I Loved a little sister above the silver lies,
Pesos stacked by others' eyes.
I Loved a little sister spinning motions stolen to entice.
I Loved a little sister
Beneath a speckled orb
Reflecting specks of lights casting shifting
Colors across the spray
That held,
Like death holds onto life,
Her short black hair in place
Beneath the brown unbobbing bottle
Balanced on her head
Above her dark-brown eyes reflecting mine
From where I stood behind the bidding crowd
Where fragments intertwined
And moments passed like cancer
As she pressed her body down.

The crowd began to wiggle
And salivate upon the meal made

Beyond the coffin lid,
And, as she did that Peso dance,
The crowd began to rip and tear
Her time the union tied with
Stranded ideals spun in darkness.
With eyes of iron and claws of gold,
They ripped away some life,
And when she rose and squeezed the lies
Into her soft brown hands,
The silver shapes were heavy,
Falling down upon the stage,
Ringing bells of Hell
Between waves of color
Cast in spinning disco flashes blinking.

When the jingling faded,
I bought her,
And we walked away, escaped
The shiny bars
That cage the meadow lark.
As strangers we were forced to meet;
The lark supposed my bed
Her prison for that night,
But I laughed,
And speckled moments sparked
When she saw the apeneck's eyes were mine,
And her mother's voice echoed
From the creek we walked beside:
"Rice for peace. Rice for peace. Rice for peace."

That evening, white grains piled high
Upon the plates between
Our eyes and misunderstandings,

Grains of rice that filled our minds
And hearts with the possibility
Of some gallant Windhover
Soaring freedom filled skies
Beyond the sights of mortal eyes,
Peace leapt from the final grain upon my plate,
Yet such faith as was reborn in those few hours
Died within,
Crucified by time on questions
Beyond the garden we have walked within.
For between the white blindings
Where holartic emotional landscapes
Filled with black and bonding what there could be
With lattice fragments full of might.

Om, Tara, through my tears,
Your visage offers a rebuke.
I fear St. Ignace,
For the moment anyway,
Has died
In those ripples wild
Between the past and this two-hearted river.

Here is a truth:
I am no better or worse than any other.
I've said and done things I
Would never have imagined myself
Saying or doing.[1]

Let us stop before we move.

---

[1] These are the words of a Nez Perce Warrior, a Vietnam
veteran left for dead after one battle. He woke in a body
bag, and some years later, passed these words to me.

Perhaps I've said too much,
Dared to eat that peach and lost at Love.
Oh, lady, shall I lie in your lap (smile)?
There now, I mean no harm beyond the strain of asking,
Which, for some, is only a fair thought or county
matter,
But for me it's the offer of my Life.
With too much at stake to fool around,
Let us rest, and let me be your jig-maker.
For what else can I do
But be merry with wishes held so deeply?

Enough of play and indecision.

Listen to the power of this river
Calling us to feel and change,
Calling while my walking stick
Speaks of bearing fruits coniferously.
Om, Tara, we could wonder at the life it must have led,
A life of standing,
A part of something growing taller,
A life of bending in the wind,
flexible,
yet locked in place.

Let's get up and move along.
This straight gray stick
Used for walking,
Is now a spirit moving far beyond where it was found.

Even here, this process of showing you the Wilderness
Shows me
My strange sense of isolation,

A Keatsian melancholy,
The feeling of sorrow needed to create
The blissful space of these few fractions bound,
A joy only fleeting,
Dependent on belief and fractions found,
A gift shared in moments passed
And passing before questions
Flow as must in mortal minds.
I am so lonely and yet so found.

Oh, River of No-Return, you are my Wilderness!
These specks of time arriving faster than my thoughts.

This stick used for walking grows heavy in my grief,
Returning me to questions governed by unknown.
See now spirits passing round us?
Watch as these steep canyon walls begin to waiver,
First at their edges,
Then melting toward the center in kaleidoscopic
transformations:
Our once revealing river, now but yellowed, muddy,
Cutting slowly through a fasting of the heart.
Let us wander these new hills.
Let me start again:
Can't you feel the joy of fish?
I know! It's in your eyes.
I started with a question that might seem foolish.
I'm simply asking that you feel my WAY.
It's all a kind of play.
O, put me in thy books!
For by this light whereby I see thy beauty
(I say it is the moonlight that shines so bright),
There is a way of living without fear or plans or sorrow,

As did the ancients,
Those who wandered as small points
Of interest in larger landscapes
With waterfalls and lakes
Where joyful fish are lost in water's deep reflections
Of two opposing forces, nature
Intertwining,
Losing form and shape,
But filled with echoes in union
With union
In a garden where the wonderings
Of the wandering (those like us)
Become a single movement flowing
In any direction
Within the harmony.
Now see another figure,
One full of notes and fragments
To alter what might become
Through order
By living
Moments as rites,
A figure that would be a man of ignorance,
A man of no opinion,
A man naming things correctly.

Look, it seems so silly, but
I wish Confucius would have drank more beer.
And I'm sure Lau Tzu
Would drink with me and you.
Because that's how we are.
At some level, Love, we are
Both Kate and Petrucho...
Well, Kate and Petrucho after the end of the story,

A Daoist couple playing well together,
Two minor forms walking beside
A mighty River,

Peaceful,
Peaceful,
Peaceful the escape
In this garden where we walk,
A garden where a master might please her or his life
By achieving *ren ai*,
By holding empathetic thoughts,
By doing his (or her) best for others
For the trust of all
By maintaining the ability
To mend mistakes
In mending ways.
But this reality always gets struck down,
Hammered
By those who follow The Prince,
(There is a part of me that wants to laugh just now:
"Beware of flatters" the author wrote.)
A prince clothed in ghastly gowns,
A prince who keeps false faith
To harness forms of power.
(It's sort of like hanging out with folks who are cool
when they're sober and assholes when they're
drinking.)
Cast him away from you!
Tara, we will watch that prince fall into the water,
Splashing, sending ripples through the flowing order,
Filling the voidless void
With military vigor,
Hidden vice, and tarnished rice.

See me now transforming!
Don't look away, though I might seem to hunger.
Watch as I become a raging tiger
Riding on a dragon above a soaring eagle
Searching for a monkey hiding from a leopard
Leaping toward a crane pecking at a mantis.
As the princely world flows away,
Climb upon my back when I am near,
And we will escape.
Hear my heart as you hold tight.
It pounds a kind of truth within my chest.
Hear my roaring clash and thunder.
And see the flash within my eyes
That does evince a flaming soul.
But fear me not
This thing I can become.
Dispel devaluation.
Oh, fly,
Fly with me
And splash through the surface of that azure sky above.
Feel your fingers clench my saffron pelt
With trust,
And smile for the moment's thrill.
Life, see the world in currents,
Currents spinning, melting,
A great tornado
Filled with colors swirling round and round and round,
A storm in which we course toward its center.
Hold on to Love as the changing swirl of Chaos
Sucks us down and down and down toward its center.

And then we rolling land upon another firming,

And dash beside the goddess, Laughter,
And her daughter, Fun.
Along that grassy path that leads us
To the edge of some other garden,
One only moments beyond the venom
Found in black and white,
A path that leads us to a place
Where truth becomes a Way,
A Way void of desire,
A middle path,
And, like other paths,
Sometimes tarnished by our sense of might
In day dependent
On the night.
Like any path,
It takes us
Down tunnels
Filled with followings
By followers
Lost between forming and deforming fragments.
But don't lose hope,
For together, we will feel our Way.
Look closely at the edges of this delicate tapestry,
And you will see
Some crawling through the roots
Still searching for direction
Beneath their apple trees,
Some screaming at lung-tops most
That this or that perception of the fragments
Our wills need follow,
Some in hopeless drinking drowning
Fragments altered to forgetting,
Some lost in circular fragments changing

Without departing,
Some blinded by nature's drive to penetrate
Whatever meal is set before them,
Some losing cause within a square of opposition,
Yet all following followers
Through thorny brushes
And rose stems
Holy only in the dark
Perfect dark
Dark swirling rose of creation
Dreamt by the Owl
In the daylight darkness of isolation,
And queried questions
Beyond the conflict rattling through my mind
Are now reminding me of this trail
Beneath our wandering feet,
A trail (to finally answer your question) where walkers
Of the past have also set their feet
And made such change as they by chance could cast.

Oh, trail stretching on and on,
Before us peaceful, tranquil, hostile, dark, and light
Changing through moments filled by questions
Between gardens we have seen and have yet to see,
Gardens filled with rosy shades
That all too soon are but falsehoods woven
Betwixt fragments intertwined, fragments
Forever captives mingling in the time
Before and beyond their original occurrences
In the mist of their unique influences,
Gardens one day ending, fading
Across some burnt hillside,
Splitting or dividing or waning,

And I must, one day in growth,
Experience, endure, or investigate
Another garden
With pathways
Where fragments unperceived are most expected,
But least assured.

Oh, Friend, I accept the fright
Of going blindly through that dark gate,
For going there will free me to find the hope of light
And shift, thereafter, your dread of leaving
Into a grand delight.

Here, by this river, Starshine, Life, and Love,
Questions are the only answers,
And gardens are forever varied.
Some hold roses while others thorns,
Yet seeing some gardens share a thread
Or carry fruits so like in kind,
I will search for fragments that guide my heart,
Search within these rules to which we're wed till death
Wherein last breath discovers truth.

I will search between the blackness
Of birth and leaves falling
And never rising from the bed
Of some last garden,
Search for that truth
Beyond the stretch of perceptions
Limited to some few fractions bound,
Perceptions more often forgotten than remembered,
Search for the flame of that rose
So hoped for in this life

That lives are made in honor of the thoughts
Of hope and faith well placed in minds
Dancing through these fragments.

Oh, there is another subtle thought:
That in the mist of fortune
Moving removed from awareness
In some sick joke of creation
There is an end,
An end allowing mortal moments
To simply fly into the void beyond,
Forgotten over time
As signals lonely in the night
Colliding with particles unknown
In some random journey,
Endless, tireless, unreachable,
Expanding with the edges
Of this grand something,
The sole product of nothing.

In one is hope of joy
Through continued perceptions where gardens
Might exist in full bloom
For time and perception,
A something that will never fail
And nothing is but the past.
In the other lies
But this fragment,
No more or less, yet lesser than the first
For more dependent on chance
Beyond control, refinement,
Or taste, looking dangerous,
Disagreeable, repellent,

As some anti-strength or power,
Destroyer of flesh vacant of soul.

If the one,
The response is Divine value;
If the other,
The response is ended fragments.

Faith no longer lives here
If such the lonely land,
For hope is all we have
To hold in bloody hands
While nails scratch
A coffin lid of slate,
For dread be all we know
In such a union
That coughs within the night
And keeps us from our sleep.

(If you look on a map, you'll see
We're not far from Cabin Creek.)

Love, above this speculation filled with fragments,
There is a hallowed resting place,

Gaze, Life,
Up, up, and up again.
See the sky, blue and dotted white with fast-moving
Clumps of clouds.
Strange that there is little breeze down here
Below this dry hillside rising from Big Creek's
V-shaped basin, here
Closer to the center of the earth.

I hear blue grass music
And lonesome Irish reels, a love supreme.
I hear the sound of your spirit next to mine.
Call it Joy of our desiring,
Like watching Bach.
See bits of bunch grass and countless talus slopes,
Heat waves rising,
And dream,
While the gardens
Of events and thoughts and people
Intertwined where fragments of the past
Break through and surface
Between the currents of our thoughts and steps
Within the echoes
And fragment-filled existence,
Dream about a cool, refreshing spring surrounded by
The iron-forged gates of "Western" thought,
A garden different from others,
So different that if somebody were to bring me
News of this sort,
I would want to know if he or she had not been
Blinded by insanity.
We will need to leave the safety of our trail for a bit.
Take off your pack, and let it rest here while we
Climb this slope.
It will sit well beside mine.
And when we return, even though we won't
Have time to rest,
At least our packs will have slept together.

Hear helicopter blades clapping against the sky
In slow-motion thumping.
A guitar and tambourine, the playing of an evening rag.

This is the end,
Beautiful friend.

This is the end
My only friend, the end

Take my stranger's hand,
And we will pass beyond that desperate land
To climb and witness a last stand.

There is a silence here.
No longer birds singing or crickets chirping.

And we must climb
Scarcely brooking the strain
Of each foot falling calling pain
Until we find a pile of rocks—
Hallowed ground.

If we get home before daylight,
We might just find some rest tonight.

Stand up!
Stand up!
Wake up!
Wake up!

Welcome to this hallowed ground
Where the curves of Big Creek
Stretch below and echo on beneath
The side of this hill so steeply banked
To meet what knowledge of myself and man

Has come to call and call me
Delirious as I start and then begin to sing a line of light.

Here's the story....
Six of us climbed to this same spot,
This spot where you and I now gaze
At that fast moving river so far below us.
At this spot
Ashes were placed
In folds of colored wool
With medicine used
Behind the sweat house door
And an eagle feather
Given to me by a Niimiipuu hamma.
Mourning my old man, the man I held as half divine,
With his drumstick, too,
And a smoke,
With sweat from climbing and tears
On rocks provided by the thoughts
Of ending thoughts,
Where after all was done,
A butterfly arose,
Gray with blood-red stripes
At wings' edges,
Flapping with clicker clacks
Like wooden sticks
Beating in ways no mortals might achieve,
And it flew around us,
Fluttering about our heads,
Brushing up and down our bodies,
In a garden of fragments,
To disappear,
To return,

To repeat, replenish, and rejuvenate,
A garden of timely fragments
Full of fragments unperceived
Provoking reason
Full of hope for that space between the crib
And that place near the grave
From beyond the place of butterflies
(Oh, Lapwai! Oh, Home! Oh, Place! Oh, Family!
Oh, longing that drives me to sanity!),
But the smiles smiled were found
In a momentary awareness
Of feeling far older than
Words like mine,
Words written in black and white,
Yet not so old
As the age of man (or woman or X),
And I was filled with awe
And mystic waves of overjoyed
As life returned anew in altered fragments.

Quid sum miser tunc dicturus?
Quem patronum rogaturus,
Cum vix justus sit securus?

Ingemisco tanquam reus
Culpa rubet vultus meus
Supplicanti parce, Deus.

Confutatis maledictis
Flammis acribus addictis
Voca me cum benedictis.

Oh, that my heart would burst!

The Bloody proclamation to escape,
That follow'd me so near (O, our lives Sweetness!
That we the pain of death would hourly die
Rather than die at once!), taught me to shift
Into a mandman's rags, t' assume a semblace
That very dogs disdain'd; and in this habit
Met I my father with his bleeding rings,
Their precious stones new lost; became his guide,
Led him, begg'd for him, sav'd him from dispair;
Never (O fault) reveal'd myself unto him,
Until some half hour past, when I was arm'd
Not sure, though hoping, of this good success,
I ask'd his blessing, and from first to last
Told him our pilgrimage. But his flaw'd heart
(Alack, too weak the conflic to support!)
'Twixt two extremes of passion, joy and grief,
Burst smilingly.

Here, within this moment
Free from pigmentation,
Organization,
Separation,
Is where I will continue walking,
Though even far from here,
Even to the point of being no closer
Than upon the echo's edge
Where missing memories forever
Remember
The trial of wilderness,
For spirits now surround me.
They know I mean no harm,
For I now
Feel the cast of moments

Dreamt before their dawn,
And the whirl of fragments guides me
Through the echoes of return
That bring us back to
The fires of our trail
Below this sacred place.

Well, I close my eyes
Only for a moment
And the moment's gone
All my dreams
Pass before my eyes of curiosity.
Dust in the wind,
All we are not is dust in the wind.

Oh, Muse, Glory of All Creation, Life, and Love,
Feel the depth of my soul.
It has felt the lashings of Hell that meld with Love,
And still, it longs for more.

Don't blush.
I'm not that kind of longing.
I'm a soulful longing, a desire to be
Connected to others' souls,
A desire to nurture the deepest overshadowing,
To make the world a better place.

To see where the spirituality of our Friendship
Might lead, we would have to ask, "Why not?"

And I think:
There will be peace when we are done.

As a Friend, for all that word is worth,
It is with you that I would now traverse.

Peace, enough of that.
Let's finish the walk, my friend.
But first, watch me bound down this hill,
Jumping like a skier in fresh snow
Down the talus slopes,
And all but fly toward the river
Which flows now loudly
So far below.

Meet 'ya down below!

And so you see me
Fading fast.
The sloping chase of my shadow's thrill
A guide to you
To follow as you will.

And when you come,
I will be there (picking up our packs),
To share,
To Blend (upper case blending),
To be your…
To be your…
To be your…
It's hard to find the words….
To be your… Time to stay.

Oh, within this wilderness surrounding me,
I can now hear
The older harmony

Exposed
By Big Creek
In rapid interventions,
And in my mind I see
All things as striving spirits
Dependent in the dream.
Still, the duration being questioned,
Like ragged claws of stone,
Rips through flesh and spirit intertwined
Between the more uncertain strides upon this trail,
Spilling blood and interweavings
Upon the ancient leaves of grass no more
Than past and gone,
Bringing a bluish hue to aging skin
And the frozen thoughts
Of some sick joke of chance
Near the end
Of Big Creek's trail
Not so distant from this place
Where my aching chest will burst,
Before my back is bent,
Victim,
Victim,
Victim
To the friction of fragments
Rushing in and out of gardens
As we walk along together,
Dreamt in isolation,
Captive,
Blinded,
Lost within the fragments
Of this vast and roaring blue-green cathedral,
Big Creek Gorge,

Where my limited awareness
Perceives only the blood-red marker
So vastly separated,
Yet so near in meaning,
To an old-time place of dreaming,
A place where smoke-stained rock
Rises out of the original harmony,
And we hear drums and voices joined
Within the echoes of Big Creek's thunder,
A majestic song,
Unexplainable,
Irresistible,
United
In this place,
A testament to those who lived here
Long before the cannons
Added the sounds of genocide
To the music heard so loudly
As an eagle glides
Between the cliffs and screams
At us
To hear His voice.
And We are He,
Watching the canyon walls
Pass within the blue blur
Of the moment and the wind
That moves around our feathers
To push us up,
Up, up, and up
Above the highest walls,
To see the speckled fish
Below,
And you and I,

You and I (like a Yes song)
Watch
As the Eagle folds His mighty wings
And falls
From the great blue above
To absorb
In talons clenched,
The fish I knew was there,
And then He (or She or We…because I see the God in
you, too)
Rises
Once again
And joins the air swiftly,
Moving between
The blood-red marker
And the place of dreams,
Rushing to the point of disappearance,
Rushing to a place where the echoes call
On me,
And the trail beneath my feet
Asks to feel
The tapping of my stick,
To hear our passing music
Meld within the fragments,
And we continue walking
My tears falling
Upon the rock,
A process adding some significant sound
To the beating or your heart within the music
Of this place, Love, A place filled
With the glory of your Being, too,
A place from which we pass without even knowing
We are gone.

Distance seems only sound
Within a blur of movement
As we progress,
As we walk along
Trying to figure out how to explain the Wilderness
To future fragments
Unknown,
Living behind us,
Drawing breaths sometimes with pain,
To tell a story
In a world
Seasonless,
Herbless,
Treeless,
A world as it would be for me without you,
A world filled with smoke and the stench
Of rotting bodies
Nothing more or less than food for dogs
Whose bellies swollen drag
Upon the pavement of ancient cities
Crumbling in the mists of time beyond
Our more mortal awareness,
And now, Life, as the waves of heat rise
From the water-fired rocks of Big Creek,
I see a bridge
Spanning the distance
Between one swollen bank and another (Mother Earth,
Tara Firma)
Where our response awaits.

Here, at the heart of the Wilderness,
While those who follow remain behind,

We set our packs and clothes upon the deck,
And hand in hand and eye to eye and soul to soul
We climb
Upon the rail of this arched gateway,
To stand balanced and looking down.
Oh, and then to leap,
To dive,
To lunge toward the ever swift below,
To swim together in this clear cold water
Where Big Creek joins the Salmon.

Om Tare Tu Tare Ture Soha

Tea Poems

Boorish Blondie

Boorish Blondie,
An apeneck slouching
In towering Tea
Temple of all-rites white,
After a couple laughs,
Grabs harshly
The thirteen-year-old cat,
Justice:
Tied up and twisted,
Permission-less petting
Preceding
Scratching and screaming,
Slobbering
Slimy lips,
Chasing and tripping,
Bleeding and crying,
Hissing fits.

Erected now
By crowds of cows,
Boorish Blondie
Muffles older Justice--
Hidden proceeds,
Threats, promised deeds--
Leads dropping
Case off Tea Tower.
Cows chew cuds
As Blondie accompanies
Justice to bottom floor.
Elevated downstairs,
Media's Extra—ordinary

Slimer
Sits flip-flop now
On Tea Throne
As ill Douche

Burning Spice

Watching "Baghdad Bob"
The Spin Spicer
(Home-sliced shyster and
Tea-bagging
Spokesman for
Old Small Hands)
Proclaim concocted
Numbers present
At THE coronation
Sometime soon
After prostituting
Cheerleaders holed up
At CIA headquarters
got the clap
Accomplished,
A remembrance returned:
Goebbels' death,
His children unburnt
In stark contrast
To his own
Pusillanimous period,
His owed demise,
Arms outstretched,
One more act
Of propaganda.

Sindone Sacrileghi

O' say can you see
Blue, white, and thee,
Tea,
Bagged, red and wrapped,
Tongue-split, twisting and strapped,
Dangling by string?

O say can you see
Old Gory
Flapping in the breeze,
A shrewd shroud wrapping
Round and round and round,
His frayed yellow fringes
Streaming…
An image profound,
No sound,
Just a cloth-shelled achene
Dunked but not drowned
In mean gasoline?

O' say can you see
My match held as the key,
A creative decree,
Well lit,
Flaming obscene,
A Tangerine
Dream?

Sweet Tea, Just for Me

Tea, baby, just for me, please,
Request
Jenson and Michell
To do their best in
Deeply vetting psycho test--
Not to wish you harmed,
No... never
That, not
To hear the
Screaming sounds
Of boiling water
Steaming thee, Tea,
No... never
That, not
To watch you
Dunked and dragged
Teabag naked,
No... never
That, not
To have you
Prison put for
Steeping,
No... never
That, not
To have your
family, friends then
Hunted down,
No, never
That, not.
Not that,
But, Tea, baby,

Just for me,
Just for all we've had
and shared,
Just for this
One week,
For banning Muslims,
For building walls,
For ceasing refuge,
For halting medication,
Sweet Tea,
Please, for me, pick
Your poison quick, pick
To swollen swallow,
Maybe almond smells,
No... never
That, not
The viper bite
On pudgy breast,
No... never
That, not.

Tea Hastened the Fall

Tea hastened
The fall
Of democracy
Now and then.
So steeped
To think
In what
Too soon became
A drowning
In stunned
Cerulean
Tones that
Presently transformed
While soaking
In the fear-filled joy
Of witnessing
The awakening,
The arising
Of an opposition
Infantry ebbing
And flowing in
Shards of
Shattered glass.

The Edict of Hospitality

The Tea is hot
And scorching,
And those who
Drink do so
Forgetting how
Odysseus taught
Disruptive political
Cocks
To gift
Refugees
And the poor
With Love,

For the gods
Will, from
Time to time,
Be of such
Ilk, and
Let not those
Who drink
This yellow Tea
Forget how Athena
Lessoned US to
Honor those
Most in need
By washing feet

Least we
Be torn from
Our perch
And dashed against

The rocks
Below, and
Let US not
Forget that
Ancient poet's
Proclamation,
Commanding us to
Treat those most
In need with
Gentle words,
Food, a resting place
Or risk our
Kingdom's fall
From grace.

The Jester Sings

Obfuscations
Within miasmata
Whiddershins swirling
Fabrications
Freakish Cabbala cantata
Subserving retaliations--
Hallmarks all of autocratic
Fornication for Tea.
Let me, Jester now,
Coxcom: Cap and Bells
Bouncing atop me vistadome
Riding Rails
Past a nation's Gloaming tell true,
"The world's all aflame... aflame... aflame!"
"Squeaky's sexing Charley in
The people's White Homestead!"

And through these gates of Darkness
Now we pass:
Why fear
Tea,
The one you called
Insanity?
The earth's still here.
So stand up upon
That Standupon!

I'll be that rooster dancing round
For Joy! For Joy! For Joy!
Take off your shoes and squeeze
The loam between your toes, for

It is fertile,
And in it you will grow:
That's the worst Stardust
(not Snowflakes melting)
That can happen.

Love...
Tis Light enough for dangling
My bells and comb
This jingle jangle morning.
Love...
Take to basking in
Its bright-lit baptizing:
No longer is there Night,
Or maybe Night's returned
But that is only darkness,
And it will not withstand
The Light...
Good morning Sunshine!
The Earth calls to US, assuring US,
That darkness will not last.

Use your jester's map.
Sing and dance and live
A revolution to the drop,
Every red drop
Returned unto Infinity.
It's blessing's past bestowed
To stand upon this loam
And digging heals in
Furrow hallowed ground.
Now, I gaily say,
Let everything you touch

Return to green,
Through nurturing or painful toil
Until you pass.
Create to see
Those others way ahead
Forgiving as they march
And waiving back for US
To follow foolishly

Lines Drawn in Land's Sand

Lines drawn in Land's sand...
See now as I plan.
Oh, you masters of war,
These lines in the Land
Will quick undermine
In swampy quagmire
The horrid foul stink--
Your elected satire.

Oh, you clowns
At the top...
You will squeak
When you pop--
Cartoons on the tube,
Though your teeth aren't
A ruse.

Ga-Daffy got his
All just
Some show biz!
Th-the that's all
That there was--
Feathers n fuzz!
We remember it well,
All a plume in a poof.

Then heard all around--
Loud quacking profound.
Oh, you masters of Tea!
You ducks and you clowns...
I'm but a gadfly

Who knocks on your door.
You might think me too chary,
But it's all in good fun.

You're at a party with children,
And I've squeezed your red tongues.

Christmas Tea

Apeneck Agamemnon,
A foolish, prideful celebration
Of abscessed possibility,
Plods about
His white house
In this Christmas
Tea poem—
Snow outside,
As dreamed of,
Cards sent in mail,
Everybody joyous in
Evening's dawning.
Clytemnestra, hidden Knavs
Near hot tub
(Not yet turned on),
Did best before homecoming,
Decorating interior
With trees,
A white forest scene
For the Ice Queen—
(Oh, the suspense
Is overwhelming!)
If only she would draw
That hot bath
For Apeneck Agamemnon,
If only Clytemnestra would
Decorate her
White trees with
Red too.

www.ingramcontent.com/pod-product-compliance
Lightning Source LLC
Chambersburg PA
CBHW070515220526
45467CB00002B/679